100

things you should know about

SHIPWRECKS

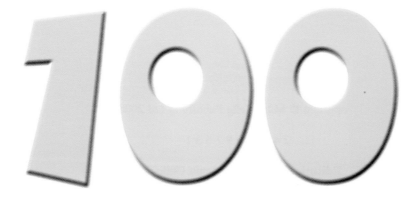

100

things you should know about

SHIPWRECKS

Fiona Macdonald

Consultant: David Parham

Miles Kelly

First published in 2008 by Miles Kelly Publishing Ltd
Bardfield Centre, Great Bardfield, Essex, CM7 4SL

C

Reprogr   Paulyn

ISBN 978-1-84236-573-1

Printed in China

British Library Cataloguing-in-Publication Data
A catalogue record for this book is available from the British Library

ACKNOWLEDGEMENTS
The publishers would like to thank the following artists
who have contributed to this book:

Julian Baker, Richard Burgess, Mike Foster, Adam Hook, Richard Hook,
Oliver Hurst, Wes Lowe, Patricia Ludlow, Andrea Morandi, Tim@kja-artists.com

All other artworks are from the Miles Kelly Artwork Bank

The publishers would like to thank the following sources
for the use of their photographs:

Cover Reinhard Dirscherl/FLPA
Pages 6–7 National Maritime Museum, London, Greenwich Hospital Collection;
9 Rex Features; 10(t) Amos Nachoum/Corbis, (b) Jonathan Blair/Corbis;
11 Jeffrey L. Rotman/Corbis; 13 Amos Nachoum/Corbis;
14 Ralph White/Corbis; 15 2005 TopFoto.co.uk;
16–17 Jonathan Blair/Corbis; 25 Terry Fincher.Photo Int/Alamy;
34 Bettmann/Corbis; 34–35 Topham Picturepoint TopFoto.co.uk;
35 David Pollack/Corbis; 36–37 Bettmann/Corbis; 37 Corbis;
38 Reuters/Corbis; 38–39 Newspix/Rex Features; 39 epa/Corbis;
40 TopFoto.co.uk; 40–41 Corbis; 41 TopFoto.co.uk; 43(t) 006 TopFoto.co.uk,
(b) Â©World History Archive/TopFoto.co.uk

Made with paper from a sustainable forest

www.mileskelly.net
info@mileskelly.net

www.factsforprojects.com

Contents

What is a shipwreck?

1 Originally, the word 'wreck' meant 'something washed up on a seashore'. Today, 'wreck' is used to describe the remains of a ship that has sunk or been badly damaged. In the past, shipwrecks were more common because more people travelled by water, and ships and navigation techniques were less reliable. Today shipwrecks are less frequent, but they still claim thousands of lives each year.

▼ In 1588, Spain sent an Armada (fleet of ships) to attack England, but it was scattered by English fireships (ships set on fire and sent towards enemies), and around half were wrecked in a storm. This painting is called *Defeat of the Spanish Armada*, and was painted by Philippe-Jacques de Loutherbourg in 1797.

How ships float – and sink

2 The Greek scientist Archimedes found out why things float over 2000 years ago. He jumped into his bath and noticed that when he did so, the water overflowed. He realized his body was pushing the water out. When ships float, they 'displace' water, in the same way.

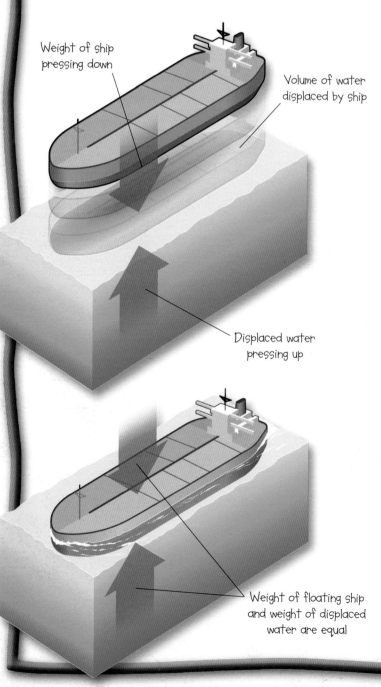

Weight of ship pressing down

Volume of water displaced by ship

Displaced water pressing up

Weight of floating ship and weight of displaced water are equal

◄ The water displaced by a floating ship pushes back with a powerful force equal to the ship's weight.

3 Archimedes discovered that water displaced by a ship pushes back on the ship with a force equal to its weight. This holds the ship up in the water. The density of a ship is also important. Density is the weight of an object measured along with its volume. If a ship or any object is less dense than water, it will float. If it is more dense than water, it will sink.

4 Ships are often made of materials such as iron or steel, which are denser than water. However, ships also contain a lot of air. Air is very light, and makes the ship much less dense than water.

Air is trapped inside
these holes

▲ Modern ships have double hulls,
which trap air between two layers of
metal. Air is less dense than water.
The trapped air makes the ship less
dense, helping to stop it sinking.

5 Ships sink when water gets inside them.
A decrease in the amount of air inside a ship makes it less
buoyant. Water gets into ships when they are holed by
rocks or guns, battered by
winds, swamped by waves,
lean sideways too far,
or overturn.

▶ If a ship's hull is holed,
water pours in. Together,
the hull and the water are
denser than water alone, so
the ship sinks. This picture
shows the oil tanker *Braer*,
shipwrecked off the
Shetland Islands, off the
Scottish coast, in 1993.

Treasures of the deep

A diver scans the seabed, searching for metal objects such as coins or cannon that will help him locate a wreck buried in the sand.

6 Wrecked ships can become trapped on rocks or be washed ashore, but more often they sink beneath the waves. They may sink straight downwards, or twist and turn for many metres before coming to rest. Then they may be crushed by water pressure, pulled apart by currents, or covered by corals, mud and sand.

Divers 'float' above the fragile remains of a shipwreck to examine them before touching or removing them.

7 Investigators search for shipwrecks in many different ways. They look for clues, such as coins or pottery, or strange, unnatural shapes on the seabed. They use echo-sounders and side-scan sonar to 'see' in dark, cloudy water, and magnetometers (electrical detectors) to locate metal objects. Sometimes, they use robots and towed vehicles to make surveys.

8 Before they dive, investigators study maps, charts, ancient books and old newspapers. They read coastguard reports and consult government records of accidents and shipwrecks. They find out about local sea conditions, such as waves and tides, as well as freak weather events such as hurricanes.

9 To reveal a wreck, investigators may make bore-holes through sand and mud, or drill through coral. Sometimes they use pumps to suck mud from above a wreck, or suck sand away with compressed air. Once they get close, they have to work much more carefully. Instead of using tools to brush mud or sand away, they uncover objects by fanning them with their hands.

◄ Divers use a float filled with air to help raise a heavy iron cannon, found at a 17th century Spanish shipwreck.

10 Once a wreck is found, its site is marked with a grid, or poles fixed at regular distances. These help investigators draw plans of the site and record the positions of their finds. Satellite measurements and photographs help record the wreck as it is revealed. All objects taken from the site are labelled, listed, drawn, examined and identified.

I DON'T BELIEVE IT!
Some divers have suggested using sea lions to help explore wrecks. Sea lions are intelligent, and can swim and dive in spaces too small or dangerous for humans to explore.

Diving discoveries

11 People have longed to explore shipwrecks for centuries. Humans can only survive underwater for a short time. They must breathe oxygen, keep their lungs free of water, and be protected from the weight of water above them and from the cold of the seas.

12 For over 500 years, people have tried to design diving suits. In 1715, English inventor John Lethbridge built his 'Diving Engine'. Shaped like a big wooden tube, it had a glass viewing panel and leather sleeves. Divers using it claimed to have explored 18 metres below the surface of the sea.

▲ John Lethbridge's Diving Engine was used in 1718 to collect treasure from the wreck of a ship in the Atlantic Ocean.

▶ Sealing the helmet and suit made diving safer – divers could now be sure of having enough air underwater. Earlier diving suits often filled with water, drowning their wearers. Versions of Siebe's design remained in use until the 1980s.

14 The 'Newt Suit' has been described as 'a submarine you can wear'. Invented in 1987 by Canadian engineer Phil Nuytten, like other ADS (Atmospheric Diving Suit) designs, it surrounds the diver with a metal shell. Inside, the diver is warm, can breathe air at normal pressure, and is not crushed by seawater. He or she can dive to 700 metres, and stay underwater for five or six hours.

13 German engineer Augustus Siebe was called 'the father of diving'. In 1840, he invented a method of sealing together a metal helmet and rubber suit. Air was pumped to the diver down a tube from the surface. In Siebe's suit wearers dived down 25 metres. They explored shipwrecks and built bridges, dams and other underwater constructions.

▶ The Newt Suit is made of strong, light aluminium. Its moveable arms and legs make it easy for divers to work or explore.

Robots and submersibles

15 Many ships sink in very deep waters. People cannot safely descend more than 200 metres without protection. They would be crushed by the water pressure, and could not stand the extreme cold. To explore deep sea wrecks, people use robots, towed vehicles, ROVs (remotely-operated vehicles) and submersibles.

▲ Remotely controlled sled ANGUS is fitted with lights and cameras to explore extremely deep seas, and is guided by pilots at sea level.

16 Robots can be programmed to carry out deep-sea investigations. Many devices allow robots to collect information about a wreck. Cameras and sonar (scanners that use soundwaves) can create images, sensors test the water, and mechanical arms pick up objects.

▼ ROV *Jason* was launched in 1988. It needs a pilot, a navigator and an engineer to operate it.

17 ROV *Jason* lets explorers investigate wrecks from sea level. The mobile unit (*Jason*) is linked to the survey ship by a cable 10 kilometres in length. *Jason* can be steered through a wreck or across the seabed, and can take photos or make and record measurements.

Lights

Manipulator arm to collect samples

Tray for collecting samples from the seabed

Sonar, used to make images of the seabed

Voyager submersible has sensor 'eyes' that produce three-dimensional images of the underwater world. Investigators wear special goggles to view the images.

18 *Alvin* was the world's first deep-ocean submersible. Built in 1964, it has completed an astonishing 4200 dives. It is a strong, watertight capsule that can carry two investigators and a pilot 4500 metres below the sea's surface. It is fitted with bright lights, air supply, viewing windows and robot arms, and is propelled by six jet thrusters.

19 Towed vehicles can be dragged through deep water by ships sailing on the sea. They are linked to the ship by cables that carry electronic signals. They are used to make maps of wrecks on the seabed, or to take microscopic video images of underwater wildlife and bacteria.

▼ Submersibles need very powerful lights, as it is pitch dark in the ocean depths. Submersibles are smaller than submarines, only carrying a few people to operate them, but they can dive to far greater depths.

The first shipwrecks

20 **The earliest wrecks so far discovered are over 3000 years old.** They are the remains of two trading ships that sailed the Mediterranean Sea between 1350 BC and 1200 BC. They were both found close to the Turkish coast, at Ulu Burun and Gelidonya. Storms had driven them onto rocks, and sunk them.

21 **Both ships' hulls had almost disappeared.** Just a few scraps of wood remained. Archaeologists had to estimate their size and shape from cargoes scattered on the sea floor. They also found clues in wall paintings from ancient Egyptian tombs showing Mediterranean ships and traders.

Carved stone seal

▼ The Ulu Burun ship carried gold and silver jewellery, pottery, brilliant blue glass, ivory, valuable ingots (bars) of copper and tin, and many other valuable items.

Wooden writing tablets

22 **Cargo on board each ship was packed in giant jars.** These huge pots, called 'pithoi', kept cargoes dry and safe. They were stacked at the bottom of a ship's hull, and surrounded by bundles of twigs for padding.

Gold medallion

◄ Archaeologists hard at work cleaning and preserving the wooden hull of the Kyrenia shipwreck.

23 Sailors on the Cape Gelidonya ship carried charms for protection. Five stone scarabs have been found at the wreck, along with the ship-owner's merchant seal. This was a little cylinder, carved with symbols, used to stamp the merchant's signature on bundles of cargo.

▼ Experts built a copy of the Kyrenia ship in 1985, so they could find out more about ancient Greek ships and how they were sailed.

24 In 1967, divers discovered wreckage on the seabed near Kyrenia, Cyprus. It was the remains of a Greek cargo ship that sank over 2300 years ago. Amazingly, three-quarters of the wooden hull remained, and was almost undamaged!

25 Hundreds more ancient wrecks have been discovered in the Mediterranean. They date from ancient Greek and Roman times, between around 500 BC and AD 500. The wrecked ships carried all kinds of valuable cargoes, from wine and olive oil to works of art – and slaves.

Viking shipwrecks

26 The Skudelev ships were discovered in Denmark in 1959. They lay across Roskilde Fjord (a long, thin bay), completely blocking the narrow entrance. They had been wrecked on purpose around AD 1000 to prevent enemy ships approaching. Their hulls had been filled with heavy stones to stop them floating to the surface.

▶ Danish Vikings sinking the Skudelev ships to make an underwater barrier against invaders. The wrecks stayed hidden underwater for nearly 1000 years.

Sunken ship on shallow sea floor

27 Investigating the wrecks was difficult and delicate. The timbers were so fragile that they could not be moved through the water. So the archaeologists built a coffer dam – like a box in the sea – and pumped the water out of it. Then they carefully lifted the wrecked ships to the surface, piece by piece.

Ship being filled with stones before sinking

28 Reconstructing the wrecks was like piecing together a puzzle, and took many years. Over 50,000 pieces of wood were found in the fjord. Each was photographed and numbered before being moved. Now they are on show in a museum.

Two ships
under water

Stern (back)
of ship sinking

Small cargo ship
carrying stones

▲ The Bayeux Tapestry, made around AD 1070 by Vikings settled in France, gives us information about what Viking ships looked like.

29 **There were five ships at the wreck site.** Two were warships, designed for raids. Two were cargo ships, built to carry traders and settlers. One was a little ferry boat or fishing boat, made for short trips in coastal waters.

30 **Ships like the Skudelev warship carried invaders.** They are pictured in the Bayeux Tapestry, a huge embroidered wall-hanging that records the Norman Conquest of Britain in 1066. Ships like the Skudelev cargo ship reached North America around AD 1000, steered by Viking explorers.

BE A VIKING

Imagine you are a Viking pirate, sailing across dangerous seas. Be like a Viking, and:

1. Choose a name for your warship – Vikings liked very descriptive names such as 'Wave-Beater' or 'Sea-Snake'.

2. Write a poem or a song, describing your hopes and fears for your voyage. Will your journey bring you fame and riches, or will it end in a dramatic shipwreck?

Medieval Europe

▲ Galleys smashed holes in enemy ships with sharp battering rams. They also hurled 'bombs' of an explosive mixture called Greek Fire.

31 The Pisa wreck was lost for over 700 years. It was a galley (a ship with oars and sails) belonging to merchants from the city of Pisa in Italy. Medieval writers described how the ship was attacked by rivals in 1277, off the coast of Ukraine. It was set on fire, overturned, and sank to the bottom of the Black Sea. For centuries, no one knew where it was, but in 1999, archaeologists found it!

32 On board was lots of fancy pottery made for rich Italian families. Italian people of the time were able to buy beautiful things imported from distant lands. Bowls and dishes found at the wreck site were made by potters working in several different styles and traditions. Some were Christians, from Constantinople (now Istanbul and Turkey). Others were Muslims from the Middle East.

▶ The big wooden hull of the Bremen cog is 15.5 metres in length. Amazingly, it was still in one piece when it was found.

▶ Combining evidence from shipwrecks with images like this medieval seal allows archaeologists to work out what the Bremen Cog might have looked like over 600 years ago.

33 **One kind of pot that was found on the Pisa wreck is a mystery.** Called a 'spheroconus', it is shaped like a globe with a spout. It may have been used to store mercury – a poisonous medieval medicine – or water from Mecca, the Muslim holy city. Or it might have been a weapon to throw at enemy ships!

34 **Few medieval shipwrecks survive.** The wood, hemp fibre and canvas they were made of has rotted away. One of the best-preserved medieval wrecks is the Bremen Cog, from Germany. It was found in 1962, by dredgers (digging machines) widening a harbour entrance.

35 **The Bremen Cog was wrecked before it ever set sail.** Around 1380, floods swept it from a ship-builder's yard. After being stranded on a sandbank, it became covered with mud and silt. This stopped bacteria from rotting its timbers.

Chinese junks

36 Chinese junks were the biggest ocean-going sailing ships in the world. We know this from Chinese shipwrecks. In 1973, a wrecked junk was discovered near Quanzhou, south China. It was 34 metres in length and 11 metres in width and could carry 350 tonnes. It had three tall masts and was five times bigger than most European ships of its time.

37 Junks had special features that made them unlikely to sink. They had bulkheads (walls), which divided their hulls into compartments. Each compartment had a watertight cover and a drainage channel.

38 The Quanzhou junk was wrecked around 1275, probably in a typhoon (hurricane). It was blown onto rocks, a huge hole was smashed in its hull, and all the compartments filled with water. Accidents like this show that even the best-designed ships cannot always survive the very worst weather.

39 **Lucky charms were hidden on junks for extra protection at sea.** Divers exploring the Quanzhou wreck found seven bronze coins and a mirror. These represented the moon and the stars – traditional Chinese symbols of fair winds and good fortune.

40 **Around 60 merchants sailed on the Quanzhou wreck.** Each had his own cabin. They were travelling with precious cargoes from Africa and South Asia, including pepper, perfumes, tortoiseshell and seashells (which they used like coins). Other junks carried spices and fine pottery.

◀ A Chinese junk, similar to the Quanzhou junk, is blown across the sea by a violent typhoon. The sailors struggle to lower its sails to reduce its speed through the water. Waves surge around the hull, but its waterproof design helps it stay afloat, unless it is holed.

Tudor ship

41 The *Mary Rose* is one of the most famous European shipwrecks. It was the flagship of King Henry VIII of England. Designed for war, it could shoot guns and arrows at enemy ships, or sail close to them so that its sailors could leap on board. *Mary Rose* sank in 1545 as cheering crowds, including the king, watched it sail away to battle.

▶ Water pours into the hull as the *Mary Rose* heels over. At this point, there was so much water inside that sinking was unavoidable.

42 Building the *Mary Rose* started in 1509. Then, in 1536, it was fitted with new, powerful cannon. Rows of gun ports (holes) were cut into its hull, above the waterline. The muzzles of the cannon pointed through, ready to shoot deadly cannon balls at the enemy.

This cutaway shows the water levels inside the ship

The water is pouring in through corresponding gun ports on the other side

▲ Slowly and very carefully, the wreck of the *Mary Rose* is lifted from the seabed on a massive metal cradle that has been specially made in exactly the same shape as the ship's hull.

43 **The weight of people and guns on the upper decks made the *Mary Rose* unstable.** Suddenly, it heeled (leaned over) to one side and water poured in through its gun ports. It could not right itself (return to an upright, balanced position), filled with water, and sank rapidly. The soldiers and sailors on board were trapped by nets meant to keep out enemies. Around 500 drowned.

44 **The *Mary Rose* came to rest leaning on its starboard (right-hand) side.** Its starboard decks and cabins sank unharmed into the soft mud of the seabed, close to Portsmouth, southern England. Year by year, layers of silt covered the wreck, hiding it completely. The *Mary Rose* became a secret Tudor time capsule.

45 **Investigators have tried to explore the *Mary Rose* wreck several times.** Soon after it sank, Italian experts tried to find its valuable cannon. Between 1836 and 1840, divers dropped explosives near the wreck to uncover it. Archaeologists surveyed the wreck in 1967, then began to excavate it in 1979. In 1982, the remains of the *Mary Rose* were lifted to the surface. Today, they are displayed in a museum.

I DON'T BELIEVE IT!

In just four years, from 1979 to 1983, archaeologists made almost 25,000 dives to the seabed to recover the shipwrecked *Mary Rose* and its contents.

25

East India ships

46 The *Batavia* was one of the first sailing ships to sink off Australia. Owned by a Dutch trading company, it ran aground on reefs between Australia and Indonesia. The dangerous seas in this area sank hundreds of similar ships, called East Indiamen, between 1600 and 1800.

47 At first, it took a year for an East Indiaman to sail from Europe to Indonesia. In 1613, Dutch captain Hendrick Brouwer pioneered a new route across the south Indian Ocean. This made use of reliable 'trade' winds, and reduced the journey time by half to around six months at sea. The *Batavia* was following this route when she was wrecked in 1629.

48 We know a lot about the *Batavia* wreck because the captain survived. He wrote a description of the ship hitting rocks – and what happened afterwards. With some officers, he set off in small a boat to seek help, leaving 268 passengers and crew sheltering on the islands. After they had left, a passenger and his friends attacked the other survivors.

◄ Strong gales and wild waves washed the *Batavia* onto hidden rocky reefs. With only wind to power their ship, its crew were powerless to avoid them.

▶ Archaeologists investigating the East Indiamen wrecks carefully record the positions of anchors, cannon – and boxes of treasure.

49
The *Batavia* mutineers killed 125 men, women and children. No one knows why. Perhaps they feared they would run out of food and water. When the captain returned with rescuers, after an adventurous voyage, the murderers were executed.

50
The wreck of the *Batavia* was discovered in 1963. It had sunk into a shallow reef and was overgrown by coral. This protected it and its contents from being scattered or swept away by waves and currents. Guns, anchors, ballast and parts of the hull all lay on the seabed in almost the same positions as when the ship was sailing.

I DON'T BELIEVE IT!

The 'trade' winds, used by ships like the *Batavia*, got their name because they always blow along the same path across the ocean.

▶ Sailors on board the *Batavia* used astrolabes to measure time and try to calculate how far they had travelled eastwards. Accurate clocks that worked at sea had not yet been invented.

51
Surprising things were found at the *Batavia* wreck site. These included a set of silver dishes for the Indian Emperor Jehangir and a carved stone doorway for the Dutch fort at Batavia (now Jakarta, Indonesia). Also found were four astrolabes (instruments used to plot a ship's position) and part of a globe showing the countries of the world known to Europeans around 1600.

Pirate wrecks

52 Spanish settlers in America sent gold and silver home to Spain, but many of their ships were robbed by pirates, wrecked on reefs or sunk by hurricanes. Only two pirate shipwrecks have been found. One is the *Whydah*, the other is the *Queen Anne's Revenge*.

53 The *Whydah* was launched in 1715 in London, England. It was named after the West African port, Ouidah (pronounced 'Whee-dah'). It was 31 metres in length, and needed a crew of 146 men. The *Whydah* was captured by the pirate Samuel Bellamy, known as 'Black Sam' because of his dark hair.

▶ Pirate captain 'Black Sam' Bellamy was only 29 years old when he drowned in the wreck of his ship *Whydah*.

BE A PIRATE

You will need:
square of bright red cloth

1. Fold the cloth in half.

2. Stretch the long side of the cloth across your forehead.

3. Tie the points of the cloth at the back of your head. Now you're ready to sail the stormy seas!

▶ Bellamy's loot, stored on the *Whydah*, included 180 sacks of gold and silver jewellery and bullion (pieces of gold and silver metal), and more that 100,000 gold coins.

54 Heading home to London in 1717 after its second slave-trade voyage, the *Whydah* met Bellamy. He chased it for three days then captured it. He then sailed the *Whydah* northwards, along America's east coast, robbing 53 ships he met along the way. The pirate crew on the *Whydah* came from many different lands including Britain, America, Africa and the Caribbean.

55 The *Whydah* sailed into a storm off Cape Cod in 1717. It was battered by 112-kilometre-an-hour winds and 9-metre-high waves. Bellamy tried to steer the ship away from the shore, but it hit a sandbank. It overturned, and smashed into pieces. All but eight of the crew drowned. When the survivors got to shore they were arrested and six were executed for their pirate crimes.

56 The *Queen Anne's Revenge* belonged to the pirate Edward Teach. He was known as 'Blackbeard' because he wore burning fuses under his hat to surround his face with smoke. In 1718, Blackbeard and his crew attacked the port of Charleston, South Carolina, USA, but were chased and fought by a British Navy ship. Blackbeard was killed, and the *Queen Anne's Revenge* sank near Charleston.

Ships' graveyard

57 The seas around Cape Horn, the southern tip of South America, are the wildest in the world. Fast currents, rocky shores, thick fogs, icebergs, roaring winds and massive waves up to 30 metres high make sailing difficult and very dangerous. There are 78 known wrecks charted at Cape Horn itself, with at least 800 more in the seas nearby.

CHILE

ARGENTINA

ATLANTIC OCEAN

FALKLAND ISLANDS

PACIFIC OCEAN

Ships' graveyard

Cape Horn

▲ The seas around Cape Horn and between Cape Horn and the Falkland Islands became known as the 'ships' graveyard' because so many great sailing ships were wrecked there.

58 Why did sailors and ship-owners risk these dangerous waters? To make money! In the early 19th century, before railways were built in the USA, the quickest way to reach California was to sail round Cape Horn. In 1848, gold was discovered there. The next year, 777 ships sailed round Cape Horn, carrying eager gold miners.

◀ The ships that raced around Cape Horn were fast 'clippers', with slim, streamlined hulls, up to 12 metres wide and 60 metres in length. Clippers needed big crews – about 50 men – to handle their massive sails. Steering clippers was a skilled and exhausting task.

I DON'T BELIEVE IT!

A sailor who had sailed round Cape Horn was allowed to wear a gold hoop in his left ear. Some sailors said grimly that the gold would pay for their funerals.

59 In 1912, the British sailing ship *Cricceth Castle* set sail from Peru towards Europe. It was loaded with guano – dried sea bird droppings, which were to be used as fertilizer. As the *Cricceth Castle* rounded Cape Horn, its rudder was smashed in a storm, letting water into the hold. This mixed with the guano and blocked the ship's pumps completely. The hold flooded, and the *Cricceth Castle* sank. Only seven sailors survived.

60 Clipper ships also sailed from Australia and New Zealand. They carried wool, grain and gold to Britain. In 1890, New Zealand clipper the *Marlborough* was wrecked on its way to the Scottish port of Glasgow. The next year, another clipper crew saw the *Marlborough* on rocks near Cape Horn. They sailed closer, and saw skeletons on board! The *Marlborough*'s crew must have starved to death after their ship was wrecked.

Civil war wreck

61 Between 1861 and 1865, the USA fought a civil war. Northern states fought Southern states over trade and slavery. Important battles were fought at sea, as Northern ships blockaded (closed off) Southern ports to stop the South selling its produce. Many ships on both sides were wrecked. One of the most famous was the Northern 'iron-clad', *USS Hatteras*.

I DON'T BELIEVE IT!

One year after it wrecked the *Hatteras*, the *Alabama* fought another Northern warship. The shells it fired failed to explode and just bounced off the enemy ship's hull.

63 New materials were used to build the *Hatteras*, as well. It was called an iron-clad because its 60-metre hull was covered in thick iron plates, designed to survive blows from exploding shells and firebombs. Its paddle wheels were also made of iron, and so were its engine and boilers.

▼ The ship that wrecked the *Hatteras* was the *CSS Alabama*. It was one of the the most famous, and deadly, ships of the Civil War. As well sinking the *Hatteras*, the *Alabama* captured over 60 Northern trading ships. Most were set on fire, then sunk.

62 The *Hatteras* was a new ship, driven by a new invention — steam power. Coal-fired boilers below its deck heated water to make steam. This steam powered an engine that turned two large wheels, one on either side of its hull. These drove the ship through the water.

64 In the Civil War the *Hatteras* was fitted with five cannon. It patrolled Southern state coasts, capturing seven Southern warships. In 1863, it sighted a sailing ship and hailed it. The ship said it was British, and invited the *Hatteras* crew to visit. The crew launched a boat, climbed in, and then the mystery ship fired its cannon! It was a disguised southern warship. In spite of its plating, *Hatteras* was holed, and sank in 13 minutes.

65 The wreck of the *Hatteras* has survived with very little damage. Unlike earlier wooden ships, its iron hull, boiler and paddle-wheels have not rotted away or been devoured by wood-eating ship-worms. Divers discovered its wreck around 1970. Since then, the greatest threat of damage to the *Hatteras* has come from oil-drilling rigs nearby.

▲ As soon as he recognized the trick played by the *Alabama*, the captain of the *Hatteras* gave orders to fire his ship's guns. He was too late – the *Hatteras* was already sinking.

Ocean liners

66 The *Lusitania* was a luxury ocean liner owned by the Cunard shipping line. Built in Clydebank, Scotland and launched in 1906, it was designed to carry passengers between Britain and New York. In 1907 it won the prestigious 'Blue Riband' award for the fastest Atlantic crossing.

67 In 1914, Britain and Germany went to war. In 1915, the German Embassy in the USA warned travellers that Germany would treat all British ships as enemy targets. The Germans would even attack passenger ships, like the *Lusitania*, that had nothing to do with the British army or navy.

▲ Survivors crowded into small lifeboats look on in horror as the mighty *Lusitania* sinks beneath the waves.

68 The Captain of the *Lusitania* believed that it was safe from attack at sea. It could travel much faster than other ships, even German U–Boats (submarines). Surely, nothing could catch it?

▶ The sinking of the *Lusitania* was headline news around the world. Readers were shocked by the massive loss of life, and by the attack on unarmed civilians.

71 Just 18 minutes after it was torpedoed, the *Lusitania* sank. Of the 1959 people on board, 1198 died. People around the world protested at this murder of civilians. A few months later, the German government called off all submarine attacks.

69 By chance, the *Lusitania* sailed close to a German submarine off the south coast of Ireland in May 1915. The submarine fired one torpedo. It hit the *Lusitania*, destroying its controls and causing an explosion. Seawater flooded in and the *Lusitania* heeled over.

70 There were 48 lifeboats on the *Lusitania*, but only six reached the sea. Many could not be launched because the ship was tilting over. Some lifeboats were damaged by huge rivets fastening parts of the hull and others overturned as sailors tried to lower them.

▶ The US government used images of drowned women and children to encourage men to enlist (join the army or navy) to fight against Germany during World War I (1914–1918).

ENLIST

Fred Spear

35

Bombs and torpedoes

72 From the early 20th century, ships faced new dangers. Bombs dropped from aircraft, shells fired from enemy ships, and torpedoes blasted through the water by invisible submarines could wreck ships almost instantly, or cause deadly fires or explosions on board.

73 The British warship *Edinburgh* was sunk on purpose by its own navy. In 1942, when Britain and Germany were at war, the *Edinburgh* was sent on a mission to bring 4.5 tonnes of gold from Russia to Britain. It was attacked by German torpedoes, and disabled, so to stop the Germans getting the gold, British warships fired on the *Edinburgh* and sank it!

▶ The largest US warship to be attacked was the battleship *Arizona*. Weapons stored at front of the ship received a direct hit from a Japanese bomb, causing an appalling explosion in which 1177 people died.

74 The Japanese raid on the American base at Pearl Harbor, Hawaii, was a turning point of World War II. Pearl Harbor was the main United States' naval base in the Pacific Region. Without warning, the Japanese attacked it, sinking 18 US ships and destroying 188 US aircraft. After this attack, the USA joined Britain, France and their allies to fight against Germany and Japan.

75 The attack on Pearl Harbor took place on 7 December 1941. American ships and planes were attacked by 353 Japanese aircraft, launched from six aircraft carriers patrolling the Pacific Ocean. The planes dropped high-explosive bombs, designed to smash through warships' armour plating. At the same time, five Japanese midget submarines fired torpedoes towards American ships from underneath the sea.

▼ The wreck of the USS *Arizona* can be seen as a ghostly shape through the clear water of Pearl Harbor. The large white building is a memorial to all who were on board.

76 The raid on Pearl Harbor caused terrible loss of life. In total, 2388 Americans and their allies were killed and 1178 were injured. Today, the dead are honoured by a fine memorial, built out at sea above the wreck of the sunken US battleship *Arizona*. It lies undisturbed, as a peaceful grave for war victims.

Shipwrecks today

77 Computers, electronics and scientific design make today's ships safer than ever before. Wrecks still happen though, often through human error. In 2002, the ferry *Joola* sunk off Senegal due to overcrowding. Over 1900 passengers died. In 2007, the *Pasha Bulker* (bulk carrier) was washed ashore in a storm in Australia despite shipping advice to seek safer waters.

I DON'T BELIEVE IT!

In 2004, a British warship was deliberately sunk to create Europe's first artificial reef. It will be a sea life refuge and a training ground for divers.

78 Mechanical failures still cause tragedies. In 1994, the ferry *Estonia* sank in the Baltic Sea, after locks failed on its bow visor (lifting door) and water flooded in. In total, 852 passengers died. In 2000, the Russian submarine *Kursk* sank with all its crew trapped on board because an experimental torpedo misfired. In spite of efforts to rescue them, all the *Kursk* crew died.

◄ Spills from shipwrecks can kill. Sea birds' feathers become matted with oil, so that they can no longer swim or fly. Fish and other sea creatures are poisoned, and beaches polluted.

► The wreck of the massive *Pasha Bulker*, grounded on an Australian beach. When huge craft are shipwrecked, it can be very difficult to refloat them.

79 Shipwrecks can be good or bad for the environment. Since the 1990s, old ships have been sunk on purpose to create wildlife habitats or training grounds for deep-sea divers. At the same time, wrecks of vast supertankers such as the *Prestige* have threatened ecological disaster.

▼ In 2002, the *Prestige* was wrecked off Spain. It was carrying 20 million gallons of oil, almost 25 percent of which spilled into the sea.

80 Politics and war still wreck ships today. In 1985, the *Rainbow Warrior*, sailed by environmental campaigners, was wrecked by an explosion while preparing to protest against nuclear tests in the Pacific Ocean. In 2000, a terrorist suicide boat bombed US warship *Cole*, in Aden harbour, Yemen. The *Cole* was badly damaged and the terrorist boat was destroyed.

81 World poverty causes disasters at sea. Since 2000, many refugees from Africa have set sail in boats to reach Europe, and poor Asian migrants try to reach rich countries like Australia. Lots of boats get wrecked, and passengers drown.

Survivors and rescuers

82 Shipwrecks can make great stories – if you survive to tell your tale! In 1815, the *Commerce*, a merchant ship from the USA, was wrecked off West Africa. The crew swam ashore, but were captured and made to work as slaves in the Sahara Desert. They managed to escape, and when they got home, they wrote a book about their experiences. It became a bestseller!

▶ The *Endurance* was trapped by ice as the ocean froze at the end of the Antarctic summer. Its hull was crushed between ice-floes.

▼ On Elephant Island, Shackleton and his men built a camp, using their boats as shelters. They survived on food they had managed to save from the wreck of the *Endurance*.

83 In 1915, the British ship *Endurance* was trapped and crushed by ice in the South Atlantic Ocean, close to the South Pole. This shipwreck left Antarctic explorer Ernest Shackleton and his crew stranded in barren, freezing terrain. For 10 months, they camped on the ice, until the *Endurance* finally sank.

84 Shackleton and his crew faced certain death unless they tried to leave the ice. In April 1916, they set off in three small boats, and reached tiny, remote Elephant Island, off the coast of Antarctica. From there, Shackleton and five brave sailors set off across the wild, stormy ocean, heading for South America.

85 After 16 dangerous days, Shackleton and his men reached South Georgia, 1300 kilometres from Elephant Island. They scrambled ashore, and trekked overland to reach a small port used by whaling ships. Once they had recovered from their adventure, they returned to rescue their shipmates. Once safely back in Britain, Shackleton was a hero.

86 The steamship *Admella* hit rocks around the south coast of Australia in 1859. In sight of land but surrounded by raging seas, it sank in 15 minutes, leaving 108 men, women and children clinging to rocks. Rescuers took over a week to reach them. By that time 89 people had died from hunger, cold, thirst, exhaustion or falling into the sea. Only 19 survived.

▼ Shackleton left most of his crew behind on Elephant Island. They were furious, and feared that they would die, but all of them were rescued. Amazingly, no one on Shackleton's expedition died.

Shipwreck stories

87 Tales of shipwrecks have been popular for centuries. One of the first to be written down was the *Odyssey*, in ancient Greece, around 800 BC. It tells the story of a brave Greek hero, Odysseus, who survives witches, giants, monsters — and shipwrecks — on his way home from fighting a war.

I DON'T BELIEVE IT!

Stories of the Kraken — a huge sea-monster that wrecked ships — may have been based on giant squid from Viking waters.

▼ On his travels, Odysseus and his shipmates were surrounded by the Sirens. These were beautiful, half-women, half-bird monsters that sang sweetly, trying to lure sailors towards deadly rocks where their ships would be wrecked and they would drown.

◀ This dramatic poster for the film *Poseidon* shows a huge ocean liner being rolled over by a massive wall of water, stirred up by a violent storm.

89 **Many famous films feature shipwrecks.** Classics such as *The Cruel Sea* (Ealing Studios, 1953), portray the the bravery of sailors facing drowning. Adventure films, such as *Poseidon* (Warner Bros. Pictures, 2006) tell stories of ships that are wrecked by freak natural disasters, such as giant ocean waves.

90 **The exciting story of a shipwrecked sailor, *Robinson Crusoe* was written by Daniel Defoe in 1719.** It tells how Crusoe survived alone on a desert island, building a house from wrecked ship's timbers. The book was based on the real adventures of Scottish runaway and pirate Alexander Selkirk, who was marooned (put ashore as a punishment) on a Pacific Ocean island in 1704, then rescued in 1709.

88 **This shipwreck poem is scary.** *The Rime of the Ancient Mariner*, written by Samuel Taylor Coleridge in 1798, tells the tale of an old sailor who shoots an albatross (sea bird) that flies beside his ship. As a punishment, he is shipwrecked and endures terrible hunger and thirst. He is also tormented by nightmare visions of 'slimy things' that 'crawl with legs upon the slimy sea'.

▶ In Daniel Defoe's story, Crusoe is washed up on the shore of a wild, uninhabited island, the only survivor of a terrible shipwreck.

43

Shipwreck mysteries

91 Many ships are wrecked far from land, and some are never found. People try to explain these disappearances with stories. The strangest concern the 'Bermuda Triangle', an area of the Atlantic Ocean where over 500 ships are said to have been wrecked mysteriously.

▼ The mysterious Bermuda Triangle is said to stretch from the island of Bermuda to the Florida coast of the USA and the north Caribbean region.

92 The Bermuda Triangle is rumoured to contain time warps, extra-terrestrials and UFOs. It is actually no more perilous than any other stretch of water. However it is very busy, so many ships are wrecked there by hurricanes, powerful waves and strong currents.

93 Sudden freak waves off the tip of South Africa are thought to have caused many shipwrecks. In 1909, the Australian steamship *Waratah* disappeared there, without trace. All 211 passengers on board were never seen again. After several searches, the *Waratah*'s remains still have not been found.

94 In 1974, the *Gaul* sank suddenly in icy weather off Russia. It was a large British trawler. People thought that the *Gaul* might have been sunk by the Russian navy for spying, or dragged to the bottom of the sea by a Russian submarine. In 2002, a survey of the *Gaul*'s wreck showed that it had probably filled with water in rough seas after waste hatches had been left open.

ATLANTIC OCEAN

BERMUDA

FLORIDA

BERMUDA TRIANGLE

BAHAMAS

CUBA

DOMINICAN REPUBLIC

1 In 1812 the *Patriot* vanished off Florida. It was probably sunk by pirates. All the passengers disappeared.

2 In 1864 the *Mari Celeste* sank near Bermuda.

3 In 1918 the warship USS *Cyclops* disappeared. The disappearance is believed to be the result of a storm or enemy action, and the entire crew of 306 were lost.

4 In 1921 the *Carroll A Deering*, a five-masted sailing ship, was found abandoned off Florida. It was probably attacked by rival smugglers.

5 In 1963 the massive tanker SS *Marine Sulphur Queen* disappeared off Florida. However this was not really surprising, as it was badly maintained and unseaworthy.

95 The strange case of Dutch cargo ship *Ourang Medan* was reported in 1947. Other ships said they heard a wireless message from a man on board who claimed to be dying. They hurried to the place off Malaysia, where the ship was sailing, and found the entire crew, plus the ship's dog, dead on deck. A fire was burning in the *Ourang Medan's* hold. Soon, it exploded and sank.

▶ Wreck investigators think that the *Ourang Medan* was carrying secret weapons, probably poison gas, that leaked out, killing the crew.

QUIZ

1. How many ships have been wrecked in the Bermuda Triangle?
2. What caused the *Waratah* to disappear?
3. Where was the *Ourang Medan* wrecked?

Answers:
1. Over 500 2. A freak wave 3. Off Malaysia

The most famous shipwreck

▼ The *Titanic* was 269 metres in length and 28 metres wide. It was propelled by two massive steam engines, powered by 29 steam boilers.

96 The most famous shipwreck is the British ocean liner, RMS *Titanic*. When it was wrecked in 1912 it was the largest, most glamorous passenger ship ever built. It had restaurants, a swimming pool, squash courts and a ballroom.

97 *Titanic*'s designers said it was 'unsinkable'. The hull was double-bottomed and it had bulkheads, but these were shorter than they should have been to make extra space for first class passengers. This meant water could pour over the top of them and sink it, if a big enough area of *Titanic*'s hull was damaged.

98 The *Titanic* was wrecked on its first voyage, from Southampton, England, to New York, USA. Many rich, famous celebrities were on board. Most of them died, along with many other passengers. Only 712 of the 2232 people who sailed on *Titanic* survived.

99 The *Titanic* crossed the Atlantic Ocean at top speed. Late one night, off the coast of Canada, it struck a small iceberg. At first no one worried, but the hull was badly damaged and water soon gushed in. In just three hours, 'unsinkable' *Titanic* vanished beneath the waves.

▶ The *Titanic* sank in very deep water. It was rediscovered in 1985 by French and American explorers. They found out that it had broken in two before sinking. Its hull had then been crushed by water pressure, scattering debris over the ocean floor.

1. As compartments fill, the bow (front) starts to sink

2. The stern (back) of the ship begins to rise and the bow sinks more

3. The rising stern causes pressure between the third and fourth smoke stacks

4. The weak spot causes the stern of the ship to break off

5. The stern rests in the water before sinking. The sections came to rest on the seabed some distance apart

100 Shockingly, the *Titanic* did not carry enough lifeboats to save every passenger. Only 20 boats were on board. Some were launched half-empty, others were fatally overcrowded. The remaining passengers were either trapped on the *Titanic* and went down with it, or leapt into the water, where they drowned or died from cold.

Index